<u>Go Out and Sell Something!</u>

The Recession-Proof Guide to a Successful Sales Career

Rollis Fontenot III

Go Out and Sell Something!

The Recession-Proof Guide to a Successful Sales Career

By Rollis Fontenot III

Published by Rollis Fontenot III

Edited by Melanie Votaw

Printed in the United States of America

www.GoOutandSellSomething.com

ISBN 13: 978-0-615-29441-4

ISBN 10: 0-615-29441-3

Table of Contents

Introduction

The Recession-Proof Guide to a Successful Sales Career

A very popular saying is that the only constant is change. Our economy and the job market continue to fluctuate, but many salespeople thrive through the ups and downs of the economy. What's their secret? They maintain tried-and-true strategies, and they maintain the proper mindset.

And that's what this guide is all about. It is designed to help you navigate your journey toward success in the wonderful career of selling, regardless of the economic climate.

One major advantage of a career in sales is that successful salespeople are the first to be hired, the last to be let go, and are among the highest earners in the company.

Instead of trying to reinvent the wheel, I have decided to take the most relevant concepts and compile them into one short, easy-to-use guide. You'll find a

"Recession-Proof Action Plan" at the end of most chapters that is designed to give you actionable items to implement as soon as possible. Please perform every action item in order to dramatically increase your desired results. You should read this guide thoroughly at least once and use it again and again during the different stages of your sales career.

My Own Journey

I entered the wonderful world of sales in 1988 selling men's clothing in Orange, Texas. After that, I gained experience selling a wide variety of products and services, including contract work, water filters, electronics, appliances, and automobiles.

It was 1996, however, when my dream machine and personal development quest really started. I joined a network marketing financial services firm and was exposed to great personal development books like *Think and Grow Rich, How to Win Friends and Influence People, The 7 Habits of Highly Effective People, Mastering the Art of Selling*, and more.

I continued to work in the financial services field selling insurance, annuities, mutual funds, stocks, options, bonds, and alternatives investments for eight years. Three of those years were with the largest brokerage firm in America at the time with 12,000+ reps and more than $1 trillion in assets.

My ultimate growth came, however, when I went to work for a physician recruiting firm in the Houston area. At the time I was there, it was a wonderful, family-oriented, techno-savvy, pro-personal development recruiting firm. They helped hospitals and medical organizations address staff shortages by supplying medical providers on a temporary or permanent basis. I became the #1 recruiter in our company of seven recruiters.

After moving into management the following year, I have enjoyed leading a recruiting/sales team of 12 at this firm for the past 4 years. I was fortunate enough to have been able to help my department grow FIVE-fold within those four years.

I was truly blessed to work with a great group of individuals. We quickly became a force to be reckoned with in our field and enjoyed the ride!

I have recently embarked on a new chapter of my life as a sales coach and am excited as to where this will lead.

My wife and I have lived in North Houston for ten years now. We enjoy volunteer work, traveling, and exercise. My wife is a Pilate's instructor and personal trainer.

I hope that the simple principles that I have discovered throughout my sales career and present to you in this book will touch your life in a positive way, as many others have touched my life throughout my career.

Chapter 1: The BE-DO-HAVE Principle

Most people make the mistake of focusing almost exclusively on actions or DO-ing the right thing, which is why they fail.

In order to be the best, you have to BE the best. What does this mean? To be truly successful, it is more beneficial to change your thinking or being first than to change your behavior or actions first.

A principle that's very prominent in the majority of success literature, including the Bible, is, quite simply: BE-DO-HAVE. In order to get the results you want to HAVE, you must DO the things that are necessary for success, and these things are usually preceded by the correct thinking or BE-ing.

You have probably heard someone say that a person they know is just "going through the motions." This suggests that the person is missing the right motivation and thinking for the actions to be successful. There are many jobs that will allow you to be reasonably successful by just "going through the motions," but sales is not one of them.

If you know someone who became successful by focusing on the DO-ing first, it is because they began to develop the correct thought process (BE-ing), maybe without even realizing it, by repeating the steps necessary for success. We set ourselves up to always be broke and shift from sales job to sales job until we figure this one out. Sometimes, knowing why and when to take a particular action can make a major difference in producing the desired result. The right action, or DO-ing, almost always follows the correct thinking or BE-ing.

Here is what is necessary in order to develop the right thinking or BE-ing.

1. Determine your desired result or chief definite aim.
2. Become aware that a change in thinking is necessary.

3. Constantly seek new information on the changes needed in order to improve your thought process.
4. Be willing to make the needed adjustments in your thinking.

This concept is expressed in the Bible. An experienced leader named Paul encouraged an up-and-coming leader named Timothy to...

"Meditate on these things; give yourself entirely to them, that your progress may be evident to all. 1 Timothy 4:15 (New King James Version)

Notice that the positive change or progress comes from deep thought and meditation, total immersion in what needs to be accomplished, and THEN the outward changes or desired results will be reached. This is an ongoing process.

Recession-Proof Action Plan:

1. *Formulate a long-term written game plan of the results you want (due within the next 24 hours.)*
2. *Read and/or review it at least four times over the next seven days.*
3. *Read positive non-fiction or personal development literature for at least 15 minutes every day.*

Make the commitment to yourself to implement these actionable items, and use this book to help you follow through on them.

Here are two books that can help you improve your thought process. You can order these in print or audiobook format:

Think and Grow Rich (Updated for the 21st Century) by Napoleon Hill

This book focuses mainly on how to identify your chief definite aim and adjust your thinking to help make it a reality.

The Seven Habits of Highly Effective People by Dr. Stephen R. Covey

The first three habits deal with the thought process and are part of what Dr. Covey calls the private victory.

Chapter 2: Why Write Your Game Plan?

If you write a plan in the next hour, you will be ahead of most people walking the earth. Many of us have read that a very small percentage of the overall population has determined their goals and even less have written them down. If you ask how many people consistently follow a clearly defined goal-setting process, we're talking about far fewer people. Maybe 1 out of 100 or less follow a system.

As an experiment, try asking ten people these questions (telling them that you're conducting a quick survey.) Document your responses in one notebook:

1. Do you have specific goals that you plan to achieve over the next 5-10 years?
2. Are these goals in writing?
3. Are your written goals clearly defined with the desired result and steps to reach the goal, along with a specific deadline for each goal?

What kind of results did you get? How many out of ten said "Yes" to questions 1, 2, and 3? If the statistics that are thrown around today are correct, 0 or 1 answered all 3 questions with a "Yes."

This could prove to be good news for you since having a clear written game plan can help to catapult you to the top 10% of the general population. This is possible because you're willing to make the needed adjustments to your thinking and to refine your process for achieving your chief definite aim.

Writing your game plan does several things for you:

1. Gives you a visual affirmation of your chief definite aim. Reading your plan out loud is a very beneficial exercise to focus your mind on the task at hand.

2. There's a price to pay for any worthwhile goal to be reached. Going through the process of formulating and writing out your

goals helps you to discern the effort, resources, time, etc. that will be needed to complete your mission.

Jesus said at Luke 14:28: "who of you that wants to build a tower does not first sit down and calculate the expense"?

3. Having an expiration or due date gives your mind the right perspective on the time remaining to attain your goal. This holds especially true when the goal(s) are less than one year away.

Bill Bartmann was a guest speaker at a Tom Hopkins boot camp I attended, and he made a point that had a tremendous impact on helping me attain my goals. He said to stop calling our most important objectives "goals" and call them "promises" instead. Why? Most people reach their goals about 70% of the time, while they keep their promises more than 90% of the time. In addition to calling them promises, he made sure to have an expiration date on each set of promises. If we just write down "in five years," the five years becomes a perpetual date that just keeps getting pushed back another five years and becomes a goal that we never attain.

Using Bill's philosophy, I wrote my most important "Promise Plan" items. I also attached an expiration date to every item on the list. This concept was a major contributing factor to my success as a salesperson, as well as a manager.

Recession-Proof Action Plan:

1. *Formulate a long-term written goal or promise plan of the results you want over the next:*
   a. *90 days*
   b. *1 year*
   c. *5 years*
   d. *10 years*
   e. *20 years*
2. *Each promise should have a specific expiration date, such as June 1st, 2014.*
3. *Share your plan with someone you trust who will offer emotional support and accountability.*
4. *Read and/or review it at least four times over the next seven days.*

Chapter 3: Keeping Your Promises

Much has been said and written about the importance of an "exit strategy" when starting a business relationship or venture. But it's even more important to develop the habit of making and keeping promises—whether to ourselves in our "Promise Plan" or to others. And in order to keep promises, we have to work through obstacles to reach our objectives.

"Let us not become weary in doing good, for at the proper time we will reap a harvest if we do not give up." Galatians 6:9 (Today's New International Version)

The habit of keeping or breaking promises or commitments starts early in life and continues to manifest itself throughout adulthood. It's very easy to over-commit and under-achieve, especially when we're habitually accustomed to doing so. On the other hand, it's very difficult for a person who has the good habit of keeping his or her word to avoid feeling guilty for breaking it.

Don't "Try." People who overuse the word "try" are often accustomed to failing. If you're really counting on someone to do something very important for you, and they say, "I'll try," what do you think? Do you have confidence that they will actually do it for you? Probably not. The word "try" is destructive when it involves important matters because it implies that the task is either not very important or is an unrealistic goal.

Avoid using the word "try" in such situations because it sends your subconscious mind the wrong message. Using this word tells your subconscious that your main goal is not to be successful but only to make an attempt. Your subconscious mind will prevent you from being successful and will only make a slight effort to fulfill the directive.

No Escape Plan. Another way to see a commitment or goal to its completion is to avoid giving yourself a "Plan B" or "Escape Plan." If you have a way out, you have already planned to fail.

To illustrate, let's look at the example of marriage. I understand the logical or legal reasons for a prenuptial agreement, but it can have a devastating effect on a marriage. Often, more energy, effort, and deliberation are spent on the wedding day and the prenuptial agreement than on the marriage itself.

Long lists of tasks and to-do items are compiled. Expert advice is sought from wedding planners, caterers, florists, printers, fashion consultants, cake designers, books, and magazines. And depending on the amount of money available, attorneys and other experts are sought for prenuptial arrangements.

Despite all of this, divorce is a popular option that 50% or more of couples choose within the first few years of matrimony.

Why? There are many answers, and each situation is unique. But the root cause is that at least one of the two parties didn't make "keeping their commitment" a priority. They let other pursuits or interests crowd out time for their mate and were eventually able to justify breaking the commitment as a result.

It's no surprise, then, that couples who have a profound respect for the sanctity of marriage have a much greater chance of staying together. When both spouses share the common belief that a commitment to happiness in the marriage is necessary to please their Creator, success is more often the result.

Effort, energy, and thought need to go into the daily practice of remaining happy in a marriage. If you're married, here is a quick and effective action item:

Read the following statement every day: "I am happily married to (your mate's name.)" You will start to see small improvements within 30 days if you say this with feeling every day. It's very difficult to stay angry with your mate when you read those words. It's more difficult to say an unkind word to your mate, too. It becomes easier to reflect on the reasons why you love your mate and easier to overlook faults, accepting your spouse for who he or she is.

Career Commitments

Similar efforts in your business and sales career will bring the same kinds of beneficial results. Affirmations like "I am happily married to ..." are very powerful. But to be effective, an affirmation must have three essential characteristics:

Personal. Affirmations are the most effective when they are personal to you. Generally, they should begin with the word "I."

Present Tense. The word "am" or some other present tense verb should follow "I" in an affirmation.

Specific. Affirmations lose power when they are vague or broad. For example, it isn't enough to say, "I am successful." Instead, it must be something like, "I'm a successful salesperson whose gross sales consistently rank in the top 10% in my industry and #1 in my company." Or "I earn $250,000 a year as a successful salesperson."

Of course, affirmations alone are not enough to ensure success. Just as a marriage requires care and tending, you have to put in the actual work of learning your trade well. Start by honestly assessing where you are now, and put in the daily work to get a little bit better every day. A 1% increase each business day exceeds 20% in just one month! If you continue at this same pace over a 4-5-month period, you will have improved by 100%!

If you can stay focused by enjoying the small successes on a continual basis, great results will manifest over time.

What Can You Measure?

Of course, it's much easier to focus on your small successes when they're measurable. What can you quantify in numbers? This will allow you to truly track your progress over time. There will be no guessing as to how you're doing. You'll know exactly, and it will spur you on to keep your promises and commitments.

For example, in my firm, we saw our sales skyrocket when I closely measured and communicated to my team members how many presentations we made to clients. Over time, my focus moved to measuring and communicating other less important activities. Can you guess which activity went down in the process? We went from averaging about ten presentations per week to about eight presentations. Our sales dropped by 25% on a three-month lag.

Why? Because I had changed the focus from our presentations to less important matters. After noticing the devastating effect this had on our sales, I quickly moved back to focusing on presentations. We restarted our focus on presentations by emailing the whole group with the number of presentations done on a daily and weekly basis.

I created a short daily minute meeting in which each individual set two tasks for the day, such as the goal of making three presentations, sending out two information packets, etc. Each day, we recognized the person who had given the most presentations the previous day with a show of applause.

Our results were phenomenal. Some salespeople increased their presentations from 3 to 10, and later, from 10 to 15. Within the first month, almost every salesperson in our department had at least one week with more than 20 presentations. Our department's presentation numbers went up to over 12 per week on average. Our sales and profitability increased significantly almost immediately. I'm sure that our sales would have dropped even more had I let the negative trend continue. I learned a valuable lesson: Keep focus on the measurable activities that bring results, and never get comfortable.

This example also shows the importance of having a way to measure the most important activities and using that tool religiously. When you can quantify results in this way, you can take pleasure in the small victories and continue to grow and improve.

Recession-Proof Action Plan:

1. *Set two tasks for yourself tomorrow that you will definitely fulfill. Make sure you follow through until they are complete. It is better to set the bar low in order to help ensure success.*

2. *After you have been successful with the first two tasks for several days, add additional tasks to your list for the following week. You are developing the habit of making and keeping commitments.*

3. *Stop using the word "try" unless the task is unimportant.*

Chapter 4: Overcome Your #1 Enemy!

In the field of sales, there is no shortage of reasons to justify why we are not successful. **The simple fact is that each of us is our #1 enemy when it comes to achieving success as a salesperson.**

We suffer from a lack of self-confidence, stemming from childhood and past failures. We worry needlessly about the prospect we couldn't sell rather than placing our energies on the prospects who *will* buy.

We tell ourselves all sorts of untruths about ourselves, our abilities, the economy—you name it. However, what we tell ourselves has a big impact on how successful we become.

If you tell yourself that you will not be successful, it will almost certainly soon become a self-fulfilling prophecy.

Are You Listening to What You Say?

It has been said many times that it's best to "let it all out," "just be honest with yourself," or "acknowledge the facts." But is this true? Allow me to test this theory.

Wherever you're located at this moment, look around you. In order to get where you are right now, did you have to vocally acknowledge anything? Did you have to let anything out before you could start reading this book? On your last driving trip, however short, did you have to verbalize any of the obstacles on the way before you could continue, such as passing a car or maneuvering through construction?

Of course not! It would be ridiculous to verbalize these things out loud as they happen, especially to yourself. Verbalizing the obstacles doesn't change the reality, does it?

This is even true of our personal challenges and internal difficulties. There is no tangible benefit to verbally acknowledging certain things unless it's for a specific and useful purpose. Below are some examples of what a useful purpose would be:

- To encourage or uplift another person.

- To warn another person of possible or impending danger.

- To communicate with someone (including yourself) for the purpose of finding a positive solution.

While I'm not advocating that you hold in your emotions to your detriment, most of us tend to complain a lot and create negative circumstances around us. It's a bit of an epidemic, and it does none of us any favors.

In other words, if you're not using your tongue in the right way, it can be very destructive to you. Of course, this also applies to negative thoughts. Don't forget about *The Power of Positive Thinking* by Dr. Norman Vincent Peale. Positive thinking truly is powerful!

Here is a short list of non-useful or harmful verbal acknowledgements or thoughts:

1. I can never get a break.

2. I wonder what else could go wrong.

3. It probably won't work out.

4. I was never good at this.

5. I hate this part of the job.

6. I don't like this client.

7. He probably won't buy anything from me.

All of these statements send the wrong message to your subconscious mind. By saying such things, you're asking your subconscious to fulfill undesirable wishes. In essence, you're teaching your subconscious too much about what you *don't* want instead of what you *do* want.

So, when you catch yourself making these kinds of statements, replace them with positive affirmations. You don't have to immediately believe the affirmations. Remember that you're "training" your subconscious mind. You're creating a belief in the affirmation statements over time as you repeat them. This is the true power of positive thinking!

Here are some possible ways to rewrite the previous negative statements. These are written in a general way, so don't forget to make them personal and specific to you:

"I can never get a break" becomes "Things always work out well for me" or "I will have a great day today and will make __ sales or contact ___ new prospects."

"I wonder what else could go wrong" becomes "I wonder what great thing can happen for me today."

"It probably won't work out" becomes "It [specify what it is] will work out well."

"I was never good at this" becomes "I'm very good at this [specify what this is]."

"I hate this part of the job" becomes "I find enjoyment in every aspect of my job."

"I don't like this client" becomes "I find something to like in everyone I meet."

"He probably won't buy anything from me" becomes "This prospect will buy from me."

Get the idea? If you begin to pay attention to the statements you make and your recurring negative thoughts, you will see that you have your own lines that you repeat habitually. Begin to become aware of them, and turn them around to the positive.

It can be tough to change your thinking because it's habitual, but awareness is the key. Over time, you'll find that you catch your negative thoughts more and more often or catch yourself when you make negative statements to your friends and colleagues. As your awareness increases, you will begin to stop yourself before making the statement, and a gradual change will take place. You'll be amazed by the results!

Recession-Proof Action Plan:

1. *Cease complaining or stating anything negative unless you are seeking a solution.*
2. *Ask someone you trust to point out to you every time you use negative language or complain.*
3. *Take a negative statement that you have used in the past, and write it down, rephrasing it in a positive way.*

Chapter 5: Why Is It So Important To Read Positive Literature?

Unlike a physical workout that can take one to two hours, the brain workout only involves 10-15 minutes a day.

Reading or listening to positive literature edifies you and is a relatively small task that pays enormous dividends if done consistently and meaningfully.

1. Reading positive literature mentally exercises your mind to process new ideas and rekindle old ones that are of value.
2. Reading positive literature counteracts negative or neutral influences such as: TV, radio, and other forms of entertainment, as well as friends, family, your job, etc.
3. Reading positive literature helps you to counteract your own habitual negative thoughts and statements, changing your mindset.

For example, if you multiply the 15 minutes a day that you read times 365 days, you will get 5,475 minutes. Divide that 5,475 minutes by 60 minutes, and you come up with over 91 hours of positive literature reading per year. That's very powerful!

"You are the same today you'll be in five years except for two things: the people you meet and the books you read." **Charlie Tremendous Jones**

There is a wise saying and a recipe for success found in Psalms 1:1-3 that shows the importance of reading positive literature and avoiding negative influences. It tells us that if we're able to avoid taking and following bad advice, while clinging to the good advice and rules of our Creator through reading His Laws on a daily basis, we become like a tree planted near a stream of water that becomes fruitful and strong. Notice the benefit in the last part of verse 3, where it says, "and everything he does will succeed."

Please note the style of reading it suggests in verse 2. It says "in an undertone," which means that we read audibly in such a way that only we can hear. We were designed with a subconscious mind that listens to everything we say. Therefore, reading and saying the words feeds both the conscious and subconscious mind at the same time.

For an in-depth discussion of how the conscious and subconscious minds work, please read the book, *The Power of Your Subconscious Mind* by Dr. Joseph Murphy. Some of the concepts are a little out there, but a large portion of this book makes perfect sense.

Reading positive literature is an absolute must to help you grow into the salesperson you want to be and to achieve the life you want.

So, just what is positive literature? Nonfiction books, magazines, videos, or audio books that have the potential to help you improve your life. This would include the books on sales, personal development, or biographies of successful people you would like to emulate in at least one area of your life such as personal finance, business, motivational, negotiation, etc. I will suggest a few more of these books in a later chapter.

The Bible is full of nuggets of wisdom for your sales and business process, especially in the books of Proverbs and Ecclesiastes. Psalms, and what is commonly known as the New Testament, are also packed full of personal development ideas and principles.

In addition to reading the Bible daily, here are some authors that I have personally enjoyed:

Personal Development: Stephen R. Covey, Brian Tracy and Napoleon Hill

Sales: Zig Ziglar, Tom Hopkins and Jeffrey Gitomer

Negotiation: *Let's Get Real or Let's Not Play* by Mahan Khalsa

Recession-Proof Action Plan:

1. *Commit to read at least one page of positive literature per day.*

2. *After several days, increase your commitment to 15 minutes per day.*

3. *Obtain a positive non-fiction audiobook to listen to in your car.*

4. *Keep the radio off in your car for at least 15 minutes per day in order to meditate on the day's activities.*

Chapter 6: The "No Matter What" Strategy

The level of success you achieve in your sales career is highly dependent upon whether or not you subscribe to what I call the "No Matter What" outlook.

Aren't you glad your parents used this strategy when they taught you how to walk? Your parents didn't decide to give you 90 days to learn how to walk. No, they decided to teach you how to walk until you walked.

We should be just as determined in our sales careers. We must develop the thinking that we will keep working, keep pushing, and keep looking for new answers until we are successful. In essence, we're determined to be successful "no matter what." This concept takes your "Promise Plan" one-step further.

In order to become a truly successful salesperson, you need to look at sales as your career, not just your job. As a job, sales can be the lowest paying hard work there is, but as a career, it can be one of the most rewarding opportunities available—personally, professionally, and financially.

Making the decision to become successful in this or any career is the first key to achieving that success. It may sound simple, but most people try hard for a month or two to see what happens instead of deciding to keep working until they're successful.

Sales is much like sports in that it takes a willingness to study and improve your craft. This will involve quite a bit of practice and studying to join the ranks of the best.

The promise and commitment that you make includes sticking to your plan to become a successful salesperson, and that means as successful as you're capable of becoming. It means learning from your mistakes, triumphing over obstacles, and striving to be the best you can be.

Too many people try lots of things but never reach their full potential because they give up as soon as it becomes difficult. Then, they move on to something else, only going so far until they feel it once again becomes "too hard."

Most things worth achieving have elements of difficulty. There are challenges that have to be met and problems that must be solved. This is part of what helps us to learn, grow, and find out what we're truly capable of accomplishing. If everything were easy, we would be terribly bored, wouldn't we?

So, stick with it. Make that promise to yourself that you will keep at it "no matter what."

Recession-Proof Action Plan:

1. *Write down one milestone that signifies success in your current sales position and make the decision to reach it no matter what.*

2. *Share this milestone goal with someone you love.*

Chapter 7: Closing the Sale

Much is said about how to close the sale, and much of it is very useful. However, in the end, it's useful only if what you're offering is in the best interests of the buyer/customer.

If what you're offering is a quick fix and not in the best interests of the buyer, it will be to your detriment, not benefit. So the true closing of the sale starts at the very beginning of the sales process, from the very moment that you meet the prospect for the first time.

A true sales professional works to close the sale from the initial introduction to the final closing. A good salesperson uses trial closes throughout the qualifying and presentation process and continues to look for positive feedback throughout the sale.

You must learn to embrace objections and negative responses given by the prospect, because each one can help you to close the sale if they are addressed to the prospect's satisfaction.

Here are the components of most sales:

1. Initial greeting/introduction.
2. Qualifying/Questioning to find out the potential client's needs.
   a. Trial closes are woven throughout this process.
3. Presentation of products/services that are in the best interests of the client.
   a. Actual close is attempted to finalize the transaction.
4. Addressing any of the client's concerns or possible objections about moving forward.
5. Close is attempted again to help the client move forward to own the product or service.

The consultative selling approach calls for at least a two-step process in closing the sale. This means that components 1 and 2 are part of the first appointment or call, and 3 to 5 are completed on the second appointment or call.

Smaller ticket items on the retail sales floor and on the phone are typically done in one sales appointment or call. There are exceptions to either approach, of course. You probably already have an idea what works best in your industry. I suggest that you go with the flow and not reinvent the wheel. If your colleagues and competitors are using the consultative approach, for example, it's probably best to do the same.

Whether using the "one-and-done" approach or the consultative sales approach, it should follow the same basic structure or formation every single time. It should be mapped out and predictable. There are typically three to four common concerns or objections to each question or statement. You must learn the best answers to each of these in order to close the sale.

"I'll think about it…"

"I want to talk this over with my wife/husband…"

"Your price is too high..."

"I want to do some shopping around..."

I learned some great closes from Tom Hopkins and Ziglar's material and have picked up others along the way. I highly recommend their books on closes, and, of course, there are countless others you can research on www.amazon.com.

I have learned to use a combination of several closes throughout the years, but one of my favorites is the "If I could, would you..." close. It allows you to isolate the objection and create a hypothetical circumstance where the objection no longer exists. This gives you the opportunity to explore if the objection given is the real objection and if it's truly the only thing between you and the sale.

For example, if the client wants to delay owning your product or service because of not being willing to pay more than "X" for it, you can say: "I understand; thanks for your feedback. I'm not sure if it's possible, but if you were able to purchase this product from us for "X", would you be willing to purchase it today?"

If the prospect's answer is "No," you will need to do some more digging to find out the real reason why the prospect is not buying from you. If the answer is "Yes," you now have an opportunity to move toward closing the sale.

Perhaps your product has a benefit that the prospect has not considered in the value equation, or maybe you have some negotiating room, especially if a competitor is involved. Perhaps there is some option that the prospect can live without which will allow you to lower the price, or you can add an additional product or service in order to justify not lowering your price.

An effective close helps to either close the sale or isolate the real obstacle to closing the sale.

Recession-Proof Action Plan:

1. *Write an outline of your typical sales process.*

2. *Write down one close that addresses a common objection that you encounter when asking for the sale.*

Chapter 8: Selling Hollywood-Style

Actors do something regularly that salespeople rarely do but should. Actors practice their lines and role-play many, many times before they attempt to go in front of the camera!

Have you ever found yourself very engaged in a movie and feeling the emotions of the character on the screen? You might have even found yourself angry at a character, wanting to see him or her get what was coming to them. Or have you ever found yourself pulling for the underdog who faces insurmountable odds?

Did you feel those emotions because the events actually happened? Of course not. It was primarily due to the script, acting, and direction of the movie.

When a film is engaging, the script flows and gives you just enough detail to make you understand what's happening without so much that you know everything in advance and become bored.

Sales is no different from a successful movie. You need those same three high quality ingredients:

1. Script – Written sales presentation.
2. Acting – Skillful role-playing exercises and practiced lines in order to be engaging to customers.
3. Directing – Skillful involvement of all participants toward the final goal of helping clients do what is in their best interests.

Your Script

Anticipate the top two or three responses/questions you will receive throughout the various parts of your presentation.

For instance, if you give an opening statement for your product or service, have a practiced response for "Yes," "No," or "maybe/thinking about it."

If you think in three's and have responses ready for the top three objections, this will take care of 80-90% of the situations that you will face on any sales call, whether on the phone or in person. Of course, this involves determining the top three responses for each situation that you will face in a sales presentation or negotiation.

If you're experienced in your field or industry niche as a salesperson, you should be able to quickly identify those three responses relatively quickly. If so, please write them down for each section of your presentation that could elicit a response from the prospect or potential client.

If you're relatively new to the profession of selling or new to your particular field, consult your manager and the top salesperson in your branch or company to find out the top three objections you're likely to hear. Be specific with your questions, and have your written presentation ready. Mark the spots where potential objections or concerns could come up.

Here are some examples of spots within your presentation where you could ask your manager or top salesperson for possible objections:

- When you ask the prospect for the persons that will be involved in the decision.
- When you ask the prospect for the appointment.
- When you ask the prospect for the order.

These are just a few of the areas where you will want to be fully equipped to meet the challenge of leading your prospects down the right path.

Acting/Role-Playing

Another way to get an idea of the objections you might hear from your prospects is to role-play with someone else. It gives you the chance to practice your sales presentation with different types of personalities. What questions do they have, and what objections do they give you that you hadn't anticipated?

Most importantly, role-playing helps you learn how to keep your cool in the face of objections. You'll be prepared for almost anything that a prospect could say to you, and you'll stay calm and confident no matter what.

Role-playing is an essential component of sales training. Without it, you would be like an actor trying to do a scene without any rehearsal. When you know what you're going to say to most any objection, and you know how to deal with very resistant prospects, you won't be nervous during sales calls. And that's the kind of confident, at-ease person that everyone wants to do business with.

Directing

When you're selling to an individual, you also need to sell to all participants involved in the purchase of the product or service.

For example, a salesperson selling a car to a family with two children will need to involve everyone in the process of helping them "own" the car. If the salesperson only directs his attention to the husband and doesn't direct an appropriate amount of attention to the wife, this is an example of poor *direction* of the sale. It will no doubt end in the wife cutting the sale short with no hope of the salesperson closing the sale.

Ignoring the children can also either reduce the chances of closing the sale or could be an untapped resource for closing the sale. Learning the children's names is very helpful if their names can be skillfully used in the sales presentation. For example, I learned to keep a fair amount of eye contact with both husband and wife when making a presentation. When one of the two became quieter than the other, I periodically asked the quiet one an involvement question like "what do you think about..." or "how do you feel about all of this so far?" This kept the quiet one more involved in the process. The quiet one usually has great influence and will not be so quiet when it comes to saying "Yes" or "No" to your proposal.

In a corporate setting, a similar strategy can be used when dealing with "influencers" and "decision-makers." A fair amount of attention should be given to both. For example, the CEO of a company could be the decision-maker, but the office manager could influence which salespeople are able to make a presentation. The office manager will probably be unable to make a decision without the input of the CEO and/or the accounting department. So, giving attention to one party, while ignoring the other, will most likely kill any chance of closing the sale.

Preparing a good script, practicing role-playing, and skillful direction of your sale will give you the edge—just like a Hollywood film—and help you to get that all-important "Yes."

Recession-Proof Action Plan:

1. *Find a partner to role-play with after writing/typing your sales presentation.*
2. *Role-play for about 15-30 minutes per day for the first one to two weeks.*

Chapter 9: Take Calculated Risks

Many agree that sales is a numbers game, and that means it's necessary to take calculated risks.

What happens if you don't? You fall into comfortable patterns, and you stop challenging yourself. When you do that, your sales numbers will never increase. In fact, salespeople who stay within their comfort zone usually will see their numbers drop eventually. It may feel good on the one hand to play it safe, but it's also boring. We begin to lose interest when there is no challenge or risk.

It's human nature to want to be safe, but it's also human nature to need growth in order to stay motivated and happy. This is one of those paradoxes that we all fight against—how much do we play it safe and how much do we give in to the need to keep life (and a sales career) interesting?

Top salespeople are persistent about taking risks. They want to keep growing and getting better. They want to not only see their numbers increase, but they want to see their personal skills improve for the sheer pleasure of success.

Think about it: Most all of the innovations in the world have involved risk. If people were unwilling to take chances, we wouldn't have the airplane, the car, heart surgery, or even the telephone. No great thing ever happened without an element of risk.

When we stay in our comfort zone, we lose our ability to be adaptable. With so much change taking place at a rapid-fire speed, it's essential to develop adaptability skills. These skills allow you to walk into any prospect's office and handle whatever happens. You can adjust and adapt to the specific circumstances without losing the sale. In fact, the more adaptable you become, the more likely you are to take adverse circumstances and turn them into great opportunities— walking away with not just a sale but a lifelong client.

Of course, risks are frightening because they involve an unknown outcome. That's the problem, isn't it? That's also exactly why the comfort zone becomes so boring. When we remain in our comfort zone, we can almost always predict what's going to happen, and who wants a predictable life or career? So, handling risk must involve handling fear.

Handling fear doesn't mean that you stop feeling afraid. Quite the contrary. It just means that you act anyway. Fear is the biggest obstacle to a successful sales career. We fear rejection and failure, or sometimes, we even fear success. Why? Because we worry what it will be like to be truly successful. Will we have to live up to a difficult standard? Will others expect more of us?

Acknowledging that you're afraid can be very effective. Fighting it keeps your energy involved with the fear, while simply accepting it allows you to notice it, keep going, and focus your energies where they need to be—on your prospect.

But what kinds of risks should you take? Knowing which risks are reasonable and which are not come with training, practice, and experience. Learn from other salespeople, and learn from every experience you have. If you do, then every risk you take will give you the reward of a lesson, whether or not you make the sale.

And that brings up another important point. Your primary goal may be to close the sale, but a secondary goal should be simply to learn something for the next sales call. Are you going to allow a "No" or a bad experience with a client to make you afraid of taking risks? These experiences will certainly give you a better idea of the types of risks that make sense for you, but don't let them paralyze you with fear. Evaluate what went wrong, learn the lesson, and move on. Don't obsess about mistakes. The reward of the risk in this case is the lesson, not the sale, and that's truly a big reward. Everything you learn can be applied to the future. That's true growth, and that's what risk will bring you.

So, even if you feel a risk backfires on you, it doesn't necessarily mean that it was a bad risk. Decide if the risk you took was a bad idea entirely or if you can finesse it a bit to make it more viable with the next prospect. No matter what, you will come out ahead in some way, and a risk may even bring you a reward that you never imagined.

Recession-Proof Action Plan:

1. *Write down a calculated risk that you have taken in your life.*

2. *Write down a calculated risk that you have taken in your career.*

Chapter 10: "No" Usually Means "Not Right Now"

Most all of us, especially salespeople, hate to hear the word "No." Think about the great lengths we go to avoid hearing it. But I encourage you to embrace the word "No" because during a sales presentation, it doesn't usually mean "No" at all. It actually means "Not right now."

The prospect is really saying, "I'm saying 'No' right now, but with more information or different circumstances, I would be happy to reconsider."

Perhaps you could build more value by drawing attention to how your product or service will benefit your prospect. Maybe there is a promotion or attractive financing terms that you can offer to get your client closer to a "Yes."

On the other hand, when you've heard the word "No," it's important not to push too much in that moment for a "Yes" unless you're offering new and relevant information. If you do, you're falling prey to what is called "high pressure" sales—a practice that's highly discouraged because it's generally ineffective. In fact, it could turn off your prospect to such a degree that there will never be any chance of making a sale with this person.

Another useful tool is to skillfully utilize questions to find out: what the prospect liked about your product or service, how the prospect feels your product or service compares to what they have now, and what the prospect dislikes about your product or service. Don't assume that you know the answers to these questions without asking the prospect because being wrong will probably lose you the sale altogether.

Why it is good to hear the "No"?

It may not seem like it, but there are distinct advantages to hearing the word "No." The number one reason is that it is proof that you are alive and well in the game of selling. Those who don't hear the word "No" are either not in sales or are on their way out of sales, and those who don't hear the word "No" often enough will ultimately fail. It's simply a necessary part of the business of sales.

But there are three additional reasons why it's good to hear the word "No." First, each "No" gets you closer to a "Yes" depending on your average closing ratio. In his training, Tom Hopkins suggests quantifying how much a "No" is worth in your business. You can do this by figuring out the total number of "No's" that are needed to get to a "Yes." For example, if you need to talk to 20 people to get a "Yes," that means you need to hear 19 "No's" first. If a "Yes" translates to a $500 commission, each "No" was worth $26.31.

Second, a "No" gives you an opportunity to ask the prospect if they purchased a competitor's product or service, if their needs changed, and/or why they chose not to buy from you. This can be extremely helpful to you in the future, especially if it gives you ideas about how to improve your approach or gives you information about what your competitors are offering.

Third, hearing the word "No" allows you to temporarily cross this prospect off your list and allow another business opportunity to take its place for follow-up purposes. It essentially eliminates needless maybes or opportunities that are in a pending status. Many salespeople find themselves easily consumed by maybes or opportunities that drag on in pending status while their competitors are picking off their business.

It's good to remember that your stiffest competition isn't always your competitor. It's whatever your prospect was already doing before you contacted them to fill the need that your product or service can fill. This is especially true, of course, if your product or service is something the prospect has never used before. Then, it's up to you to show your prospect how and why they need your product or service. How will it make their business run more efficiently, save time, or save money? Why is it indispensable to them?

People generally like to do what's comfortable and avoid change, if possible, even when change is for the better. So, embrace the idea that often, your greatest competition is whatever your prospect was doing before you introduced them to your product or service—even if what they were doing was nothing at all.

When most people choose to do something different, however, it is for at least one of the two following reasons: to gain pleasure or avoid pain. This is universal. Of the two, avoiding pain is more powerful. It is human nature to avoid pain at all costs. Learn to be adaptable and cater toward one or both reasons in your presentation.

Recession-Proof Action Plan:

1. *Write down two to three products or services your prospect owns or is using before using your product or service.*
2. *Calculate how much each "No" is worth in your field.*

Chapter 11: Order-Taker vs. Persuader

Every one of us has persuasion skills. We learn these very early as children when we try to persuade our parents to buy us a particular toy or let us stay up a half hour later. We use these skills as teenagers to get our parents to let us borrow the car or go to a concert. We use persuasion in college to get dates. We use the art of persuasion in every area of our lives on almost a daily basis.

Salespeople, however, must take persuasion to a new level. The art needs to be studied and not performed in a haphazard fashion. We can't rely on strictly intuitive skills. We need to learn how to persuade intelligently and effectively in order to make sales.

There is a huge difference between being an order-taker and being a persuader. In order to be successful as a salesperson, each of us has to become a professional persuader. The reason why many salespeople are unsuccessful is not because they don't know how to communicate with clients. It's because they don't realize that an important part of being a salesperson is to persuade people to do what is in *their own best interests*.

Don't forget that in order to use your product or service, your prospect has to change something that they're doing right now. They will automatically resist this change, even if it's in their own best interests. So, persuasion on your part is absolutely essential.

For example, have you ever had a bad habit that you wanted to break? Even though you knew you would benefit from breaking it, were you able to change immediately, or did it require some effort on your part? If you're like most people, it probably took some effort and time. We usually need a catalyst, whether internally or externally, to help us realize that we need to make a change in our behavior.

This is where the professional persuader comes into play. You have to be that external catalyst which helps your prospect realize that it's to their benefit to make a change. In fact, you have to persuade them that your product or service is so much to their benefit that it would make no sense to avoid the change.

When prospecting, we are looking for potential needs, not just orders. If we get an order for the exact thing that we offer, and the client is ready, willing, and able to move forward, by all means move forward to close the sale. That's a given! But if sales was that easy, you wouldn't be reading this book, would you?

Most clients won't admit that they're looking for what you're offering on the initial call, at least not without some professional prodding. So, you must develop the skill to identify the prospect's needs, whether the client admits to the need or not.

Persuasion Techniques

How do you determine what your prospect needs? Well, hopefully, you have targeted your prospect to determine that the need for your product or service does exist. There's no need to try to sell an air conditioner to someone who lives in the North Pole. But you will probably need more specifics, which you'll get through qualifying your prospect during the initial sales call.

You must start by knowing backwards and forwards the many problems that your product or service can solve for a client. How can it help the client save time or money? How can it keep the client from losing time or money? How can it help the client make more money? Does it increase efficiency, which translates to more time and money? No matter what your product or service does, it all comes back to time or money. If it makes life easier, that will free up time. Freeing up time usually saves or makes money for the client.

Once you know everything that your product or service can do for a client, you can begin to ask questions to find out exactly how you can solve your prospect's problems, save him or her money or time, or make him or her more money.

When you know your prospect's needs, you can truly use the art of persuasion. Here are some persuasion techniques that work very well:

1. Show your prospect why he or she cannot afford to live without your product or service. What will be lost if he or she doesn't buy? How will that loss translate into lost money and/or lost time? There's nothing wrong with telling a prospect what will be gained by buying what you're selling, but if you can show that the loss is too great to risk, the sale is made.

2. Why does this work? Your prospect may not be able to imagine a better world with the gains that

your product or service can bring, but no one wants to lose, especially if it's something they already have. Don't forget that most people choose to do something different to gain pleasure or avoid pain. So, remember to cater toward one or both reasons in your presentation.

For example, car insurance may give a prospect the peace of mind of knowing that the car can be replaced, but if the prospect thinks about the possibility of losing the car without the ability to replace it, the emotions will come much more into play. Imagining such a loss will cause the prospect to want to take action.

Another way to put this is selling benefits rather than features. A feature sounds nice: This is what my product can do. A benefit, on the other hand, is more personal for the prospect: This is what my product can do *for you.*

3. There are some persuasion techniques that are so simple that we easily forget about them. These involve body language. Don't forget to smile, extend your hand in a handshake that isn't too limp or too crushing, and maintain open body language. This means to open your coat jacket when you enter the room, maintain good posture, and make eye contact. These actions show confidence, and they convey warmth and honesty.

4. Another simple persuasion technique that is often forgotten is the power of listening. When you ask questions of your prospect, really listen. It can even be very effective to briefly reiterate what was said: "So, what I'm hearing you say, Tom, is that you really need a device that will increase your staff's productivity. Let me tell you how our product can do that..." This helps your prospect to feel

heard by you, and it shows that you're truly interested in solving a problem and bettering the life of your prospect rather than just walking away with some of his or her money. Show a genuine interest in what your prospect needs, and you will gain trust.

5. When you ask your prospect a question, there may be a pause before the answer comes. If so, resist the urge to jump in. Don't become afraid that you're losing the sale just because there are a few seconds of silence.

6. If you tend to easily become fidgety, get a handle on your nerves. Wandering eyes, drumming fingers, or tapping feet signify nervousness, which can come across as dishonesty.

7. Be careful not to talk too fast, keeping your pace relaxed.

8. If your prospect is resistant to your product or service, ask questions that require more than an answer of just "Yes" or "No." This will allow you to find out exactly what objections you need to address.

9. If your prospect seems close to buying, ask questions that require only a "Yes" or "No" answer. This will prevent your prospect from coming up with new objections. For example, "Do you see how my product can prevent you from losing X amount of dollars?" If you receive a "Yes," you know it's time to ask for the sale. If you receive a "No," you have the opportunity to explain more about your product's benefits.

10. Know your competition. Overcoming objections becomes easier when you know what your main competitors are doing. How does your product or service measure up compared to theirs?

What makes your product or service better or different? What can you offer that they cannot?

This is something that you have to remain vigilant about. New competitors will come along, and your current competitors will improve their products or services regularly. Even if what you're selling has remained the same, you need to be prepared with selling points to get past the competition.

11. Never become defensive or argue when a prospect raises an objection.

12. Always follow up after a sale to make sure all has gone well and to thank your new client for their business. Ask for referrals, and always be reliable. If you say you're going to call on a particular day, be sure to do it. Deliver what you promise, and return calls promptly. If anything goes wrong, fix it right

away. You need to establish yourself as someone your client can count on. You want to keep this client for the rest of your career and get as many referrals from him or her as possible!

13. One of the best things you can do to improve your persuasion skills is to learn all you can about personality types. When you're able to assess someone's personality, you can determine what techniques will make them comfortable and which ones will turn them off.

    You can't change someone's fundamental personality style, and attempting to do so will almost definitely lose you the sale. What you can do is recognize their style and adapt your sales presentation to it. This is especially important if your personality style is different from the prospect's personality style.

Some people, for example, want just the facts. They want you to get to the point. If you spend too much time schmoozing and making small talk, you'll turn off someone with this type of personality. The opposite is also true. If you get right to the point with someone who needs some time for small talk in order to warm up to you, there's no doubt that you will lose the sale. Others really need you to paint a picture for them in order to envision how your product or service will benefit them.

So, first discover your own personality type. Then, learn to spot the personality types of your prospects quickly, and you'll have a good idea of what every prospect needs in order to feel comfortable with you. It will also give you an idea of how frequently to stay in contact with a particular client.

I have found the DISC profile to be of the most benefit for categorizing the different personalities that we encounter in sales and sales management. The four letters in the DISC sometimes have different words attached, but the overall meaning is the same. Here is how I understand them:

D – Dominant prospects are task-oriented and are used to directing others without a need for interaction or approval. "Getting things done" is more important than individual feelings. Small talk is a waste of time. They want you to get to the point quickly.

I-Influential prospects are very friendly, sociable types who like persuading or being persuaded. They welcome the input of others and feel that "it is all about the people." They take feelings into consideration when making decisions. They appreciate friendliness, and a measure of small talk is expected and appreciated.

S & C-Steady and Consistent describes those who are more concerned about the details. They like to see mountains of information and facts before making a decision. Accountants and engineers are prime examples of this type of prospect. They are not usually the main decision-maker, but they have a substantial amount of influence on the decision-maker.

The more you develop your ability to persuade, the better salesperson you will become. It isn't about developing a manipulative hard-sell technique; it's about learning how to communicate effectively to different types of people and in different types of circumstances.

Recession-Proof Action Plan:

1. *Determine your personality style, and think about the personality style of your clientele.*
2. *Write down two things you can do to appeal to the other personalities mentioned.*
3. *Formulate a cheat sheet of questions to use on a sales call.*

Chapter 12: Resolving Problems

The more productive you are as a salesperson, the more problems you will experience. It seems unfair, but it's unavoidable.

Ironically, this can be a very good thing. Some of my best clients were the ones with some issue that needed to be resolved before the relationship could grow. The great news is that you have a tremendous opportunity to solidify the relationship with your client. Here are some key things to keep in mind when resolving differences:

1. Listen fully to the problem or issue without interruption, even if your prospect says something inaccurate. Any attempts to explain or justify before you fully hear them out will only add fuel to the fire. It could also give the impression that you're unwilling to listen. Plus, you may miss very important information that could help you resolve the issue or keep

the issue from recurring with other clients.

2. Once you have fully heard the problem, ask the client what they would like you to do or what they propose is the best solution. This will surprise you, but a number of clients will say that you don't need to do anything. Simply listening was enough to resolve the issue because they just wanted to be heard. They wanted to know they could trust you to take care of it.

3. If the client has a proposed solution that's workable and is something you can fix immediately, say so. If any part of the solution isn't workable without verifying or altering something, let the client know that you will work on fixing the issue immediately. Be sure to give a specific time when you will follow up with a solution.

4. If the client has no proposed solution, come up with your own. If you cannot come up with a solution in the moment, check with the proper person or people, and get back to your client with the solution as soon as possible. If the solution is at all delayed, call your client back and give him or her periodic updates. Apologize, if necessary, to make sure your client knows you care about solving the problem and have every intention of resolving the issue as quickly as feasible.

Again, live up to your promises. Do what you say you will do, and check in with your client to make sure that the problem was solved to his or her satisfaction. The only way to keep your client is to truly serve and respond to problems the way you would respond to your own or the way you would want someone to respond to your problem. As a customer yourself, you know how frustrating it is when you receive poor service. Therefore, if you provide the best possible service and stay in touch with your client, you will develop a solid relationship with your client. He or she will rely on you for years to come and will know that you can be counted on to come through when you are needed.

Recession-Proof Action Plan:

1. *Take steps to reach out to someone in your back office or support and ask for their advice on the best way to communicate with them and ask them what support issues they most frequently encounter.*

2. *Ask yourself and them what ways we can explore to solve or alleviate that issue.*

Chapter 13:
Understand Your
Compensation Plan

Before accepting any sales position, it's highly recommended that you understand the basics of your overall compensation plan. This is especially true if you're moving from one sales position to another. It goes without saying that you should become very familiar with your compensation plan if you've already started a new position.

One of the benefits of understanding your comp plan is that it will help you to identify where the company wants you to focus.

For example, assuming all of the products you offer are of equal benefit to your client base, if your commission plan pays 5% when you sell a particular product or service versus 15% on everything else, this is a clue that your company does not want you to focus on selling the product or service that pays only 5%. This could be for a variety of reasons. Also, there is usually a bonus level that pays more when your sales reach a certain amount. This level tells you what level of production your company highly values from its salespeople.

Types of Compensation Plans

Most compensation plans fall into one of three categories: commission-only, straight salary, or a combination of the two with or without additional incentives.

Commission-Only. This type of position pays only when you make a sale, which means that the amount of money you earn is completely dependent upon your ability to close new business with either new or existing clients. There is no pay arrangement for effort or time worked on a sale.

In this type of arrangement, you will receive a percentage of the sale price or gross profit of your product or service once a sale is made. If you sell more than one thing, the percentage may not be the same for every item.

America's top salespeople love Commission-Only compensation arrangements because they usually have the most lucrative terms of payout and potential upside. It is the closest of the three types to being in business for yourself. It is often said that it is like being in business for yourself, but not by yourself. Therefore, only entrepreneurial and highly driven individuals need apply to these types of sales positions.

It is highly recommended to have a substantial amount of money saved before taking on such a position, however. It is recommended to have 3-6 months of living expenses in addition to an emergency fund. The exception to this rule would be those who either have an existing client base, who have very little overhead, or who are living with someone who can offer financial support during the initial months.

In order to attract more salespeople to apply, several organizations employ minimum guarantees of income within their Commission-Only plan. Essentially, this gives the company the opportunity to pay on effort and time spent in selling their product even when there are little or no sales that have been closed. There are three major types of minimum guarantees that exist:

Commission Draw – This is an advance, or "draw," of anticipated commission earnings. A minimum amount of compensation is paid against future earned commissions in what is essentially a loan that is in effect as long as you work for the company. You pay the loan or draw back as you earn future commissions.

For example, if your draw is $3,000 per month, and you earn $2,500 in commissions, the company will advance $500 to you that month in order to total $3,000. Suppose you earn $4,000 in commission the following month. Your commission check would be $3,500 after deducting the draw from the prior month. The problem that can materialize is if your sales fall flat for more than one month. Then, your debt can begin to stockpile and have a negative effect on future earnings. Although this method has been used the most in times past, it is used less and less today.

Minimum Guarantee – This works similar to a draw since you are guaranteed a minimum amount of compensation. Where this differs from a draw is that the compensation in lieu of commissions is not a loan and does not need to be paid back later. Most minimum guarantees are true to their name and are minimal. They are designed to protect your downside risk in a catastrophic month or when you are first starting the position. They are far below what you would earn at most other jobs working the same amount of hours, however. The main emphasis is getting your sales back up as soon as possible.

Temporary Salary – The philosophy is similar, but the amount is usually much higher than the other two options mentioned. In this case, the money does not need to be paid back, and you usually receive it for a finite period of time. This could range from three months to several years. Six to twelve months is probably the most common. The salary portion could be in lieu of or in addition to commissions earned during this period. If commissions are paid in addition to salary, the salary may end abruptly or be scaled down over a period of months. For example, the commission may decrease by 20% per month after month six and so on.

This form of compensation is the most attractive to the salesperson, but the company will be much more discerning about who they hire for this arrangement since their upfront investment is significantly larger than the other two plans.

Straight Salary – This form of compensation was rarely used for many years, but it has been employed more in the past ten years. In this age of the savvy consumer, some companies go as far as advertising that their salespeople are not paid commissions at all. This has been used in many retail environments such as department stores, furniture stores, and auto dealerships.

It is, by far, the least used method of compensation for salespeople. Many companies dislike this arrangement because it can make for unmotivated salespeople! Top producers do not like this arrangement because it severely limits their ability to earn a substantial income. This leaves the mediocre or subpar salespeople as the only interested applicants, which can make matters worse for increasing sales. It is an arrangement that offers little incentive to exceed the bare minimums.

Salary Plus Commission – This is probably the most popular and common compensation plan for salespeople. It allows for a bit of security, while also giving salespeople the incentive to continuously improve and make more sales.

It is very easy to get comfortable with having a salary, but be careful that your salary is not so high that it restricts your ability to earn high levels of commission. When comparing one plan with another, the plan with the highest salary is not usually the best for top producers. This is because by default, many of these plans with high salaries overpay mediocre or low producers at the expense of the top producers.

Does your firm offer other types of incentives, such as bonuses, a leased car, an expense account, contests, or advances?

Contests have become very popular, and the awards can be cash, vacations, or goods. These can sometimes be frustrating, however, if the same people win over and over.

A growing number of companies utilize incentive-based promotions that are rewards for reaching certain sales milestones rather than a competition among salespeople. Many companies prefer these because newer members of the sales force have an opportunity to compete with those who have more experience with the company.

It may be difficult to determine at the outset if a firm's compensation plan will be the most advantageous to you, but make a special effort to understand it in order to plan your finances. Don't leave it to chance. Understand the principle aspects of your compensation so that you can create a viable budget and avoid living beyond your means.

Recession-Proof Action Plan:

1. *Determine your compensation structure.*

2. *Learn how your commission plan works.*

Chapter 14: How to Fix Money Problems

Since the field of sales can be very lucrative and often pays out in lump sums, it may give you the impression that you have the ability to out-earn your financial mistakes. But this is rarely possible and can lead to constant frustration.

The key to fixing your money problems is not just through making more money. You have to develop the right thinking and mental discipline. Here are some actions you can take right now to help you get out of a financial rut:

1. **Write down all of your expenses from the past 30 days** (80-90%). If you don't have access to these expenditures, guesstimate your expenses for the next 30 days, and use these numbers to formulate your budget.

2. **Stop borrowing money today!** This means that you must stop spending money that isn't already in your hands or bank account. Don't count

on spending money that is "coming in" or acquiring loans based on your expected paycheck. This is a recipe for disaster. It is amazing what you can come up with once you take away the borrowing option.

3. **Reduce your monthly bills to the bone.** The order of importance is: food, clothing, shelter, and automobile. Call your cable, telephone, electricity, and credit card companies, etc. to see if you can reduce your monthly bills.

4. **Sell anything you don't need** that can bring you quick cash. You can have a traditional garage sale or conduct one online. You can sell many of your items, including your car for free at *www.craigslist.org*. Other good resources for selling your items quickly online for a small fee are *www.ebay.com* and *www.amazon.com*. You can also sell your car quickly through

www.autotrader.com, although I have had the same or better success using Craigslist.org. The advantage of Amazon and eBay is that you can sell your items without having to meet the buyer, and there is feedback from others to give you an idea if the buyer is trustworthy. With Craigslist.org, however, you will need to meet each buyer in person, and you should generally only deal in cash or an exchange of funds at a bank.

5. **Stop all monthly direct debit drafts** from your bank account, and use either a check, cash, or debit card until you get a handle on your finances. Then, you can reassess automatic debits. Never agree to pre-authorized drafts or give your bank account to creditors unless you do so with extreme caution.

6. **Mini-Emergency Fund.** Raise either $500 or $1,000 as fast as you can, and only use it for true

emergencies. This comes before any non-essentials and definitely before a Collection Agent. For example: Meet your insurance deductible, unexpected car repairs, etc. Normal maintenance on your car or home, gifts, and one-day sales do not count! They should be part of your monthly budget.

7. **Pay off debts** by using all of your positive cash flow to accelerate payments. This does not include your home mortgage, however. Dave Ramsey, the author of *The Total Money Makeover*, calls this the "Debt Snowball." After listening to his radio show and reading his book, I completed the debt snowball and finished mine in about 24 months. Getting out of debt as fast as possible can be one of the most difficult, yet liberating, things you will ever experience.

Vince Lombardi, the famous coach of the Green Bay Packers, said that there is always a price to pay to get the things you want. If you are in a financial rut, taking these steps will not be easy to accomplish, especially if you don't fully believe that they're necessary. So, in order to help you believe that these things really work, please read the stories contained in *The Total Money Makeover*. They will give you encouragement and the right thinking pattern to help you DO the right things to get on better financial footing. And that will give you a great deal of peace of mind! (I'll write a bit more about this great book in the next chapter.)

Recession-Proof Action Plan:

1. *Write down all of your expenses from the past 30 days.*
2. *Stop borrowing money today!*
3. *Reduce your monthly expenses to the bone.*
4. *Sell anything you don't need.*
5. *Stop all monthly direct debit drafts.*
6. *Start a mini-emergency fund.*
7. *Pay off debts.*

Chapter 15: How to Build Wealth and Retire on Commission

The key to building wealth is positive cash flow through living within your means and using credit sparingly. As I said in the last chapter, salespeople have the opportunity to make large sums of money in a short period, and this can lead to bad money behavior. Then, we tend to believe we can earn out this bad behavior. Although this strategy can work for the short-term, it never works on a long-term basis.

Your goal is to spend less than you make. This powerful concept is simple; however, it is not easy to follow. It is especially difficult if this is not something you learned while growing up. Many people did not have exposure to good financial role models. Therefore, the best way to help you implement this principle faster is to learn how to think like a wealthy person thinks.

Try to seek out a person who is a first-generation millionaire and ask him/her questions about money management.

If you do not have a wealthy person available to personally interview within the next week (I did not either), the best alternative is to read books that deal with this subject and endeavor to apply the concepts you learn.

Here are a few books that I would recommend you read, whether you are able to interview a wealthy person or not:

The Richest Man in Babylon by George Clason is a story based in Ancient Babylon that teaches valuable money concepts in a simple way. If you read only one book about finance, read this one!

The Total Money Makeover by Dave Ramsey is a step-by-step guide on how to implement the concepts mentioned in *The Richest Man in Babylon* in a very straightforward manner. This book is especially helpful if you have any debt.

As a salesperson who made uneven, sporadic lump sums of money on a commission basis for years, I had the tendency to believe that I would always be able to "out-earn my stupidity." (I borrowed that phrase from Dave Ramsey's Radio Show.) This never happened, however. After listening to Dave on the radio, I realized that I needed to change my thinking.

This book and Dave's philosophy is largely based on the wise saying that the borrower is servant to the lender (Proverbs 22:7.) When I started reading *The Total Money Makeover*, I was in piles of debt (cars, credit cards, etc.) After listening to the CD audiobook version of this book in January 2006, my wife and I instituted the plan and became debt-free (except for our home) by August 2008. We were able to call in to Dave's TV show in September and yell, "We're Debt-Free!" Yes, I drank the Kool-Aid and am loving it!

Rich Dad, Poor Dad by Robert Kiyosaki helps you develop the right thinking about the accumulation of wealth and is a good book to read after the first two mentioned above. It will really help you to improve your personal finances. This book is one of my top five when it comes to managing your money because it focuses first on how to think like rich people think instead of trying to copy what they do. The author does this by pointing to the example and advice from his biological father (poor dad) and his best friend's father (rich dad.)

He does an excellent job of taking you back to his childhood and describing what shaped his thinking about life and money. He learned valuable lessons from both Dads.

One of the important lessons I learned is to focus on the education from your job more than the wages you make. If you can work very hard for low or no pay, you are already on the right track to building wealth. There are many other very good concepts presented in this book, including what exactly is an asset. The CD audiobook is very easy to follow and listen to in your car.

If you're in debt, you should definitely read this *after* the others. *The Cashflow Quadrant* by the same author is another good back-up to this book.

Buffett by Roger Lowenstein allows you to delve into the mind of Warren Buffett and how he built his massive empire of profitable companies. This will help you to learn the business philosophy behind his many strategic moves.

I really enjoyed this book. It's a candid, engaging look at the life of Buffett. It helps you see both his strong and weak points, his defeats, and his triumphs. This book is not a "how to get rich" book, but it helps you to develop the right thinking in order to create sound investment and business strategies. It is refreshing to read about someone who has been committed to conduct business in an ethical manner while remaining humble.

The book will also show you how important it is to have a supportive family and supportive business partners to help you achieve your goals.

As mentioned earlier in the book, *Think and Grow Rich* by Napoleon Hill focuses on the BE of the Be-Do-Have principle and is a must-read in success and personal development literature. If you have the time, read the original *Think and Grow Rich* first by skipping the editor's comments. Then, go back and read it in its entirety. If not, you can read it all the way through from the beginning, as the updated version includes several modern stories that are extremely helpful, including more background on Mr. Hill and his struggles to get the book published.

He truly lived the principles he presents in the book. Most all of this information is useful because it is based on sound strategies. Since the book is lengthy, you might want to listen to it in audiobook format.

The 7 Habits of Highly Effective People by Stephen R. Covey is a book you will want to read all the way through and then, go back and work on each of the 7 habits individually. Dr. Covey shares the information in a practical way that can be applied to your personal life, as well as business.

The first three habits are personal and are part of private victories. The next three habits deal with relationships and are part of public victories. The last habit is self-renewal—the sharpening of the saw.

There are so many nuggets of information in this book that you will find useful in your life. The concept of P/PC productivity, interdependency, emotional bank accounts, effective delegation, and time management, among others, are covered in detail here. All of the concepts and ideas presented in the book are based on sound principles, and you will find that many of them are based on wisdom found in the Bible. This book is a must-read in the personal development genre and is one of my favorite books.

Why the Wealthy Are Different

So, just how does a wealthy person think? T. Harv Eker, the author of *Secrets of the Millionaire Mind*, believes that the rich have a particular mindset with specific characteristics. Here are just a few of the principles that the wealthy tend to live by:

1. They are smart money managers, while people who struggle with money issues almost always mismanage their money.

2. They focus on solutions rather than problems. They don't complain and play the role of the victim. They believe that they are in control of their lives. They realize that their outer world is only a reflection of their inner world.

3. They think big and seize opportunities. They refuse to allow obstacles to get them down. They don't let fear get in their way.

4. They seek out other successful people and never cease learning.

5. They are committed to promoting themselves.

How can you begin to adopt some of this wealth mindset today? If you study and implement these concepts, wealth is very sure to follow.

Recession-Proof Action Plan:

1. *Be frugal with your money.*

2. *Order one of the books mentioned above and start reading it today.*

3. *Use the 'Why the Wealthy are Different' list and apply it to you by changing the word 'they' to 'I'. Recite these words once a day for seven days.*

4. *Commit to not complain about anything for a week and have one person at work and at home to keep you accountable.*

Chapter 16: Financial "Do's" - What You Can Do Right Now

Before you begin to navigate a road trip to a place you've never been, you no doubt determine that you need three basic pieces of information: a clear idea of where you are now, your final destination, and a map to help guide you between the two points. In planning your financial future, the steps are very similar.

First, you need accurate information about where you are right now financially. What is your starting point?

Second, have a clear picture in your mind and on paper where you want to be financially in the next one, two, five, ten, and twenty years (see our template online) with day and month deadlines.

Third, you need to have a guide to follow along the way. So, let's get started with formulating your financial game plan. Here are some steps you can take right now to improve your financial situation:

Create a Net Worth Statement

Creating a list of all assets – liabilities = your net worth. Only consider assets that, if you desired, you could sell in the next 90 days for the price you estimate.

After listing and totaling these assets, list all of your liabilities. Simply subtract all liabilities from your assets to come up with your net worth.

For many people, this number will be less than $5,000. For others, it will be a negative number. For me, it was a *negative* $3,000, so don't be discouraged if yours is a low number. Feel encouraged that you now know your net worth because this knowledge will give you the opportunity to improve it.

A net worth statement is something that you should monitor on at least a quarterly basis. This concept of focusing more on net worth instead of focusing solely on income was presented to me in T. Harv Eker's book, *Secrets of the*

Millionaire Mind. As I mentioned in the prior chapter, this is an excellent book for developing the right mindset for accumulating wealth.

Since creating these net worth statements can be so subjective, here are some rules for getting realistic values:

1. **Automobile** – In order to get the most realistic value, you should look up the current trade-in value of your car at www.nadaguide.com, and make the necessary deductions for mileage, condition, etc.

2. **Electronics** – These items are usually about worth half of what you initially paid for them if they are less than two or three years old. They could be worth less if they are more than three years old because technology changes so rapidly.

3. **Jewelry** – These items are very hard to liquidate at anything more

than half of their appraised value, so I would suggest estimating their appraised value at 50%.

4. **Retirement and Investments** – You can either use your last month's statement from any bank or brokerage accounts you may have and/or look up the market value of any stocks or commodities you own.

5. **Business interests** – If you have a business, what could you liquidate from the business, or what could you sell the entire business for in the next 90 days?

6. **Liabilities** – These are debts or any ongoing payments where you have a balance beyond one month, such as a mortgage, car loans, credit cards, student loans, money owed to relatives, interest-free-for-90-days plans, etc. This does not include monthly bills such as

utilities, memberships, insurance premiums, etc.

Once you know your net worth, you can begin to formulate a game plan to live within your means and accumulate wealth. As you pay down your debt and bring your net worth into the positive column, work on developing your wealth mindset and read what the experts say about creating financial wealth. Increasing your knowledge and changing the way you think are the most important keys to a brighter financial future.

Recession-Proof Action Plan:

1. *Create your personal net worth statement and review it at least quarterly.*

Chapter 17: Should I Become Sales Manager?

If you're in sales long enough, the opportunity may come to take a sales manager position. Taking such a position could be a great move or a terrible one depending on what you enjoy most about the sales profession. If you're thinking about accepting such a position because you think that you will have an opportunity to make more money, think again. This is highly unlikely. Top producers make more than most managers and are usually the highest paid in the company other than those in C-level positions.

If, on the other hand, you're thinking of management as an opportunity to learn more about leadership and mentoring others while earning an above-average income, then it could be one of the most enjoyable and rewarding moves for you.

This is a decision that you will want to make carefully for three main reasons:

1. Organizations usually pick their best salespeople for management

even though these salespeople may not be the best managers of others or may not enjoy depending on the efforts of average salespeople.

2. Sales management usually involves giving up your whole book of clientele (or a large portion of it), so it may be difficult to go back to sales if management doesn't work out.

3. Compensation, yearly sales quotas, and growth requirements tend to change often on an ongoing basis. Meanwhile, you may have limited leverage or flexibility to adjust, since you have already given up either your entire client book of business or a portion of it and are reliant on the efforts of your sales staff.

There are many types of compensation packages available, and we will not attempt to review them all here.

www.GoOutandSellSomething.com

However, all of them will usually have a combination of a base salary plus incentive-based compensation.

Incentive-based compensation is usually based on certain goals or targets. The upside to the incentive-based component of your compensation is the upward income potential. The downside is that it is a moving target that can change from year to year and is usually based on growth from the prior year's results. Therefore, having several great years in a row will make it exceedingly difficult the following year to reach the levels needed to reach greater incentives.

So, deciding to take a sales manager position is an individual decision. Only you can know if it's right for you, but weigh all of the pros and cons carefully because going back to sales may be complicated.

Recession-Proof Action Plan:

1. *Ask someone close to you for his or her opinion on whether your personality is better-suited for personal production or management.*

2. *Ask someone you know who has made the transition from personal production to management for their opinion as to what they felt was the biggest challenge in making the transition.*

Chapter 18: The Joy of Sales

A career in sales can be very rewarding, and if you take pride in your work, constantly striving to improve and increase your numbers, you can reach heights that you never thought possible for you.

No matter the state of the economy, you can be a successful salesperson. So much of your success has to do with what you think and believe. As Napoleon Hill said:

"You can be anything you want to be, if only you believe with sufficient conviction and act in accordance with your faith; for whatever the mind can conceive and believe, the mind can achieve."

I hope this book has given you some food for thought, and I wish you all the best in your sales career.

Acknowledgements:

I have many inspirers, encouragers, and mentors to thank that have touched my life in many ways along the way:

My Creator, on whom I depend for life every day, and my wife, Jodie, who I also lean upon daily for support.

My parents, Rollis and Marietta, who gave me a wonderful start in life from infancy into my adult life. I am most appreciative for the training that both have given me. It has been of the most exceeding value.

I'm also appreciative of the many supervisors over the years who have mentored me into the business leader that I am today. Just to mention a few: Walter M. Broussard, Hubert Humphrey, Robert D. Scott, and Mike Armando.

Some of my inspirations include Jesus Christ, The Apostle Paul, King Solomon, Warren Buffett, Dr. Stephen R. Covey, Robert Kiyosaki, Napoleon Hill, Tom Hopkins, Jim Cathcart, Brian Tracy, Ron Marks, Dave Ramsey, Zig Ziglar, and Anthony Robbins.

Special thanks to my contributing editor, Melanie Votaw, who has been a special blessing to me on this project. Her insight and input have been invaluable. I'm so thankful that I had her help on this journey.

I also want to thank my entire sales team including current and past members who helped us on our journey to be one of the best sales teams in our industry niche. To name just a few that have made exceptional sales contributions to our team over the past 3 years, I would like to thank Kelly Green, Michael Walters, Patrick Luna, Kari Schneider, Tara Jones, and Michelle Tuey. I feel blessed to have such a great network of support.

There are many, many others to thank, but we will have to save something for the next book, right?

Please visit our website periodically at www.GoOutandSellSomething.com for the latest updates.